A Wake Up Call

DAN MARTINO

Foreword:

There's a song that's titled "My Tribute" and the first line, so appropriately addressed to God, presents such a valid question as the writer asks "How can I say thanks for the things You have done for me...?" I've been a Christian since age sixteen and was born into a family that went to church a lot. I've always known that we should and we are also instructed by the Word to give thanks to God for the things that He has done for us – namely providing His Son as the sacrificial Lamb that "once" and "for all", He addressed man's sinful nature permanently. I've been thankful to God for many blessings over the years, namely family, friends, a good job, security and health but this episode that basically consumed the month of September, 2014 redefined the concept of "thanking God" for me. I'm somewhat ashamed to say that I had become a Christian that did not "depend or rely" on my Creator, but would always thank Him for the outcome. That's a fairly significant disconnect. This isn't what we're called to do. We're called to rely on God the Father, Jesus Christ the Son and the Holy Spirit before we roll out of bed every morning. I sort of had some things backwards in my life and this experience was truly a revelation showing who I had become and how I needed to change. How I can say thanks...

I realized that one way of saying thanks to God for so many good things was to write this story. At every turn, this event was not about me (even though I felt the pain) but it was about God being in control of so many different things – me, Mendi, relatives, Doctors and Nurses, our church family, our Pastor – and that's why I choose to share this story. I simply want to share the good news that God is not Dead (by the way, watch the movie, it's really good...).

This story has many characters in it – but this was for real so these characters really exist and thank God, they existed in my story. My wife, Mendi was a true champ. Mendi's Mom and step-dad Wayne were rocks for us as they took care of another character, our son, Marco. Mendi's Dad, Eric and his wife Karen, both doctors and living in Austin, became a big part of the story. My step-daughter Kinsey and her boyfriend Jay provided their prayer and support always. Our church family and pastor were truly phenomenal through the entire challenge. Friends at work and in our community poured out their love and support. The surgeons, doctors and nurses also came to life not because of their professions, but because they cared. This story will share how these and many others contributed to our comfort and well-being. But, let me assure you again that this was not about "Dan" or any of the characters above, this event was about the great Physician, the mighty Healer and Creator of this universe, God.

My prayer is that this story might touch at least one person and help them through an ordeal, or that this story would help remove the scales from someone's eyes so that they can see that God is alive in us and desperately wants us in His presence always. This is a short story both in terms of length and in terms of the span of the "event". So many things happened in this life changing experience and the impact of this phase of my life will carry on forever. Others have fought cancer for years either beating it or succumbing to its' cruel fate. Many deal with the tragic loss of life that comes without warning and rattles their lives forever. Many books could be written and perhaps should be written in an effort to help self and others. Writing helps to heal the wounds and it also helps others to deal with their wounds. Paul wrote in Corinthians that defeat, struggles and illnesses are not necessarily "bad" in their entirety – dealing with the negative and coming through it strengthens us and allows us to be in a position to help others deal with the same issues. It should be looked at as a learning experience. I am glad that I learned during my relatively short set-back (perhaps I should not even call it a set-back, but rather a "learning opportunity).

I contemplated whether or not to provide my personal email address in this writing for those that might want to share comments or perhaps for prayer requests or advice. I opted not to as I don't profess to be anyone special, gifted or otherwise capable of counseling. I simply rely on God, my Father, and Jesus Christ, my Savior. That's who I run to. Yes, I have an incredible wife, family and great friends, and I do rely on them a lot, but ultimately, my reliance is on my Faith. So, no need to email me if you have a question. Ask your Creator. No need to share with me. Share with the Man who gave His life for you. Love and rely on your family for support and comfort as that is God's plan for us while we are here on Earth. But, always trust in the only One that will not fail you. If you're not sure how to reach out to God or if you are interested in learning more about your Creator, attend a Bible-preaching, God-loving, church. That, in my opinion is the safest place to start. You can also start by reading the book of John or Hebrews in the New Testament. These two particular books lay out quite clearly what Christ's mission was and who He came to serve – you and me. I pray that the God of all true healing and comfort be with you in your time of need.

DAN MARTINO

CONTENTS

ACKNOWLEDGMENTS

Normally, a paragraph or two of special thank you words would fill this area of a publication. I'd like for you to read the story first and then read the "thank you" words at the end of the book. Of course, you could just go to the end of the story now and read the words of thanks that are written. But, it would be much more meaningful to read the "thank you" words after you have read the book.

1 PAIN(S) IN THE BACK

I can remember the evening as if it were last night. It was a balmy Thanksgiving weekend close to twenty years ago when my first serious issue with my back occurred – of all things, I had simply bent over to straighten out a candy cane as we were decorating our front yard for the Christmas season. I never figured out what was wrong, but after three months or so, the pain subsided and I was back to my normal activities. Then, fifteen years ago, essentially the same thing happened with my back – this time, the pain never subsided. After trying shots, the chiropractor and anti-inflammatories, I had exhausted my options. I had to go see a Back specialist. It was quite obvious after reviewing MRI's and the Myelogram results, I needed surgery. Spinal Stenosis was the identified condition – in layman's terms, a condition where the spinal canal is too small which results in the pinching of nerves. The doctor was able to remove some bone and ligament material sufficient to provide more space to my nerves which alleviated the pinching. The relief was almost instantaneous as I can remember standing back up on my feet for the first time in the hospital and proclaiming that all the pain was gone. Great news but I did not realize that this was just the beginning.

Originally, they considered my case of spinal stenosis to be congenital in that I simply had a narrow spinal canal. The problem is that the more you operate on the back, particularly removing bone and ligament, the weaker your back becomes. So, although I obtained relief from the pain, I basically accelerated the degeneration of my spine.

Back in 2012, all my symptoms had returned and I was seeing a different Victoria surgeon. My son's last year of Youth Football and my opportunity to coach him for the sixth straight year was to start in six months. I was very anxious to get my back in shape so that I could enjoy his last year. My first surgery was in April to relieve the stenosis that was occurring again, but the doctor was not quite aggressive enough. Two weeks after that surgery, all of the symptoms had returned so in July, a subsequent surgery was done, and was of course, more aggressive as the doctor removed more bone and ligament. After a month or so of healing, it was clear that the surgery was a success and I no longer had the pain associated with the pinched nerves.

I'm actually no stranger to surgeries unfortunately. I think the count was at nine surgeries prior to this episode. I've had three knee surgeries, three back surgeries, a shoulder surgery, an elbow surgery and to top it all off, a toe surgery. Each of these surgeries all went relatively smooth and were for the most part uneventful. I'm now understanding that again, I had relied "on my own understanding" that this upcoming surgery would also be uneventful based on the past. It appears that I had put my own supposed strength ahead of God's strength.

Lo and behold, and only two years later in February of 2014, all of the pain was back. From the waist down to the knees, muscles would spasm and I was experiencing pain constantly. I was desperate for relief and after exhausting several options again, I found myself back in a neurosurgeon's office, this time up in Austin. It was with a doctor that used to practice up in Houston and then moved over to Austin. He certainly had great references and to top it off, my father-in-law knew of him. My father-in-law, better known as Pops is an Ob-Gyn doctor and practices in Austin so his reference was helpful also. The only problem is that this first neurosurgeon said that my back needed much more work than he catered to – I needed pins and bolts. Uggh. Both Mendi and I were shocked and disappointed to hear that I had disc problems, stenosis issues, and also some alignment issues and all at multiple levels. He was kind enough to refer us to another orthopedic surgeon that handled major cases similar to mine.

So, after three more weeks of pain, and a few more tests, we were talking to the man that could take care of all my problems – at least my back pain…After a few visits, it was determined that I needed some pins, bolts and a tune-up to correct problems at L2-L3 and L3-L4 in the lumbar section of my spine. The initial estimate for a hospital stay was 2 to 4 days, so having the surgery on a Thursday, 9/4/2014, I was certain to be home by Sunday. Recovery times from these surgeries vary significantly but I figured that I would miss up to a week or two at work and then would be back at it. Before we knew it, it was September 27th and we were leaving the hospital for good – 24 days versus 2 to 4 days is a clear indication that we or more specifically, I am not in control of my life, God is.

2 THE JOURNEY BEGINS

Both Mendi and I scheduled some time off (a week or so) from work for the surgery and drove up to Austin and stayed the night so we could be at the hospital at 5:00am on that memorable or shall I say infamous Thursday, 9/4/2014. The morning started off a little rocky as I had to go through the hospital I.D. bracelet process twice due to a technicality, albeit, an important one – Dan vs. Daniel – my Dad always used to say that "the boy was christened Daniel" so that's my given name. We finally made it back into the surgery preparation room and both of us were somewhat nervous about the pending surgery. A pleasant surprise was that the nurse that was assigned to prep me for surgery had the same exact birthdate as me, including the year. It cancelled out our rocky start, but only for a moment or two.

Putting metal components in a flesh and bone body is a little difficult to process but we knew this was the best option. Another hiccup that was perhaps a sign of things to come was a minor blood vial labeling error by our nurse. The hospital has great checks and balances and one detail was not checked off on the vial which had them drawing blood a second time (imagine that, two pin-sticks for the price of one).

I was already getting this feeling that we might have a rocky couple of days. I'm not the type that just goes along with the flow. If anyone is going to mess up, it will be me. I don't want anyone else messing up my day – yep, I'm a control freak. Slowly but surely, the need for control is melting away. God's in control, Dan is not (neither is Mendi). My orthopedic, Dr. T stops by for a chat around 7:00am to get an update on my symptoms and pain levels. During our discussion, he began to have a slightly puzzled look on his face and he actually said something that shocked me – maybe we should hold off on the surgery and do some more tests. I nearly passed out as I was so disappointed that he would consider this after enduring seven months of constant pain and discomfort. We talked through that issue and finally, he was confident that the surgery was a necessity. They had seen enough in all of films that significant improvement would be realized with the surgery.

So, we're back on track and back to praying. Mendi is and has always been the prayer warrior. Even at dinner time, the kids would prefer that I would pray, because if Mendi prayed, the food would get cold. I am so incredibly blessed to have a praying wife. I am a better man and Christian because of Mendi's prayers and I firmly believe that. Final preparations are made and Mendi and I say one more prayer, and I'm off to surgery.

I'm going to be up-front with you here – after surgery, and for the next several days, my recollection of events is horrendous, and almost non-existent. I've had to rely on Mendi and others to fill in some of the blanks in my memory during recovery from the first surgery. I had enjoyed a wonderful visit from some of my staff right after the surgery (that is, after Mendi clarified who came and when that actually occurred). Pam, Joann, Kazzie and Henry were kind enough to come and visit and it was great seeing them. I can clearly remember the visit now, but for several weeks, I had no recollection of them visiting (please don't let them know that…don't want them to think that I had forgotten them).

Unfortunately, I spiraled downward rapidly after the surgery. I can remember my surgeon coming by and validating that the surgery was successful and that it was undoubtedly the right thing to do. That was the good news.

The bad news was that during the surgery, while attempting to remove a sequestered (separated) piece of one of my discs, my dura was damaged causing a Cerebral Spinal Fluid (CSF) leak. The dura is the very delicate lining around the spinal canal that holds the fluid in the canal and provides additional protection for

the spinal nerves. A small piece of the disc had become attached with scar tissue to my dura and when the surgeon attempted to remove it, my dura tore and a hole the size of a raisin was allowing CSF to leak out of my spinal canal. The surgeon of course patched the hole during surgery, completed the spinal fusion process and the
Physician's Assistant stapled me up after a four and a half hour surgery (twenty nine staples closing up a six inch incision – later we determine that it should have been a zipper).

This is where I sort of check-out. One of the theories is that I had a significantly poor response to all of the anesthetics and also to all of the pain medicine. Losing CSF didn't help my condition either. By Friday, I was essentially incoherent, non-responsive at times, was not eating and in a lot of trouble physically, mentally and spiritually. By Sunday, they had determined that the patch had not sealed and that it was going to be necessary to go back in and to repair the patch. In only two days, I had reached the worst condition possible and by Sunday, Mendi was actually concerned that she might lose her husband of sixteen years. The Bible says to "pray without ceasing" and she was, along with everyone else. I'm glad they were because I was literally in a condition that I could not pray.

On we move to surgery "# 2"…

3 UH-OH, TIME TO RE-OPEN THE WOUND

Sunday, September 7th, 2014 was to be the day that all my problems would be remedied and I'd be on the rebound. Surgery was scheduled for late in the evening as we waited on the surgeon that would re-do the patch work. It was obviously imperative that the CSF leak be fixed.

During the darkest period of my life, Mendi had to muster up every ounce of energy to maintain her faith and to support me during this dilemma. To make matters worse, Mendi was battling a case of vertigo exactly at the same time that she had to be making decisions for me.

This is where things get somewhat bizarre. Pops and Karen were supporting Mendi in every way possible since they were only ten minutes from the hospital. Karen decided to stay with Mendi during her Vertigo spell, and Pops was my escort to surgery # 2. We're all proud of Pops as he served in Vietnam and then went on to become a doctor. I was in such a poor state that I barely realized that Mendi was sick and that Pops was going with me to surgery.

As you know, ISIS has been in the news for several months now. I was unfortunately in some sort of an hallucinatory state – and I was being escorted by former military (Pops) into the bottom floor of the hospital. So, how did I process all of it? Not well. My full recollection of that event was simple – I was captured by ISIS, led to a dungeon and then fought off my captives, then escaped on a bike – that's it. I wish Pops had jumped in and had given me some air support during the attack. That's all I remember from those four or five hours of my life. I truly felt exhausted as if I had just battled a dozen ISIS members. Looking back at that evening, I realize now how incoherent I was – I was in no way "in control". Someone saved me from the "enemy" and it wasn't Pops...

Anyway, they pulled the twenty nine or thirty staples and un-zipped my six inch incision and gently pulled apart the muscles again that had already started their healing process. They removed the first set of drains, did the repair work on the patch on my dura, and then sealed me up with another twenty nine staples. This procedure was supposed to get the leak addressed and allow me to get back to healing up from the spinal fusion procedure.

I woke up in the hospital room to find someone siphoning CSF from my incision. My first thought was that this was incredibly weird. I was thinking that the patch procedure went well and certainly there was no more leak. Not so. For the next five or six days, my incisions healed, I was starting to walk a bit but found myself struggling considerably with the pain and discomfort related to the two surgeries. For two days, I simply could not sit up in bed as that instantly had sent the room spinning and my stomach upside down. I was desperate for relief as this nightmare had gone on for too long for not just me, but also for Mendi.

We prayed together like we had never done before. Mendi prayed for me literally without ceasing, just like the good Word says. One night with pain keeping me up and really causing such a feeling of desperation, I literally began to call out to God for relief as if He were by my side (lo and behold, He was there). Mendi was sleeping, at least so I thought. The next morning, she shared with me another earth shattering revelation. Of all the prayers that she has heard from me over the past 16 years, she had never heard me ask God to help me until that night. This was one of my faults that was being slowly being dealt with. I had finally come to a place where I realized that I can't handle life on my own. I need God and I need His Son and I need the Holy Spirit. This experience again reshaped who I was in Christ. This was another wake up call for me.

In the midst of this desperation, two incredibly memorable, yet simple things happened – a text and a phone call. I had been receiving very little correspondence as most people knew that I was not going to be too excited about talking on the phone or sending out texts. Mendi was handling updates for everyone and prayer requests. One evening, as I laid in the hospital bed in such a pathetic state, I received a text from our dear friend Kim. When you're thirsty, you need water. When you're cold, you need warmth. When you're down, you need to be lifted up. The timing of the text and the content overwhelmed both Mendi and me. In my fifty two years on this Earth, there was no better time for this text. Here it is, in its' entirety:

Brother.... I just want you to know that we are praying for you. You don't need to worry or fear. Just focus on getting better.

I want to share this scripture with you: Isaiah 43:1-5 "...do not be afraid, for I have ransomed you. I have called you by name and you are mine. When you go through deep waters and great trouble, I will be with you. When you go through rivers of difficulty, you will not drown! When you walk through the fire of oppression, you will not be burned up: the flames will not consume you. For I am The Lord, your God, the Holy One of Israel, your Savior.....you are honored and I love you. Do not be afraid, for I am with you"

Be encouraged brother, for "by his stripes, we are healed"! You are an Overcomer!! In Jesus name, amen! Your friend, Kim

The words of encouragement from Kim and the verses that she selected to share with us were so moving that I cried. I cried because I was so moved that Kim shared God's love with us in an immense way and because of God's love that is so evident in the scriptures she sent. He knows us and loves us. He created us and knew us while we were in the womb. He knows the number of our hairs on our head. He wants us to prosper. He wants us to be with Him. How can you top that?

Kim's been attending a really special Sunday School class being led by Wayne, a good friend. Wayne's a deacon in our church but above all else, he's known for being passionate about his love for Christ and his love for our neighbors. Wayne and the gang have really been focusing on putting their faith into action – visit those in need, witness, help the poor, whatever it might be. They are undoubtedly wearing out their shoes and putting their faith into action. Helping out someone in God's name is so easy, yet we simply choose to go the other way sometimes. Listen to your heart and God will give you the opportunities to make a difference in someone's life. Kim made a difference in mine.

During this same period, I received a phone call from Pastor Jack. To fill you in on who Pastor Jack is would take a separate book. He's our pastor at First Baptist Church Inez but more importantly he's our very humble shepherd and God's servant that points us to God simply by his actions. He had been struggling with a few medical issues so he hadn't yet been able to visit us up in Austin. This phone call that he made to me was as powerful as if God had been on the other end of the phone. I believed that it was a message straight from the heart of God, through Pastor Jack's heart and delivered to me at the pre-ordained time. I had been struggling terribly with hallucinations from the medicines and my overall condition. Every time that my eyelids closed, I would either be surrounded by evil people, or be in a very dark setting. It felt like I was being attacked and I needed relief. When my eyes were opened, I was already being persecuted in a sense by the pain, the discomfort and the difficult situation that I was in. I was losing the battle with eyes opened or closed. My phone rings and I struggled to answer. It was Pastor Jack. I did not want him to know that I was losing the battle – I didn't want to let him down. Brother Jack is full of wisdom, God's wisdom, not man's and already knew what I needed to hear. He covered three things with me in around two minutes and the message will last a life time. Somehow he knew that I was fighting evil – he simply started off by saying "Dan, chase away the demons in Jesus' name". Yep, I cried again. It was a message sent straight from Heaven. He then proceeds to tell me "Dan, call on your angels and they'll lift your spirit and comfort you". How did he know that I had not been calling on God's angels for support? Lastly, he shared Psalm 23 with me. Growing up, my Dad would have us kids read one of the Psalms every evening before we ate dinner. I've read through all the Psalms a dozen times and realize how powerful a collection they are. Yet, the message that was revealed to me during that call was so different – I needed His help to fear no evil. I needed a place prepared for me. I needed to not want but simply accept what God has for me. I needed those green pastures and the still

10

waters. It was as if that specific Psalm had been written for me. I get it so clearly now. All of God's precious Word is for me and every other individual that is willing to open it. I can now share the meaning of this Psalm with vigor and encouragement with anyone. Thank you Pastor Jack for your phone call and for being a conduit allowing God's love to flow through you.

So many different people reached out and shared their prayers and love with us that it's hard to cover everyone. Both Mendi and I are so incredibly thankful for family members and friends that made it possible for us to get through this episode without any scars – the only scars are the ones on my back. Our souls, spirits and hearts are stronger than ever before and we've come through without a scratch. That was possible only through the mighty hand of God.

I recall an early visit from the Pairs and the Fowlers...dearest of friends and part of our church family. The ladies, Janis and Cindy visited with me for a while, then took Mendi out to lunch just to get her out in to the fresh air. Scott and H.E. stayed with me. It was lunch time and my appetite had still not returned and to make matters worse, the main entrée was baked fish – that was not going to work. Well, these two Godly men have served others in many ways and are great definitions of how we are to be servants in Christ. Today, they were going to take care of me. Scott was on one side at the bottom of the bed and H.E. was on the other side. H.E. grabbed my lunch plate and without hesitation, started feeding me. I was not happy...H.E. does most of the cooking on Friday mornings for our Men's Breakfast and Bible study. His middle name should be "Tasmanian". Nevertheless, with dead baked tilapia flopping all over the place, H.E. proceeded to feed me. A fifty something year old man was feeding a helpless fifty two year old man out of pure love. I saw it in his eyes that he wanted me to get better because he loved me. Scott on the other hand didn't have such an enviable opportunity to reach out and share some love. He was put on urinal duty and he did it with a smile. Here's where the story gets really neat. With all my heart and with my eyes, I felt and saw Jesus Christ himself sitting in the window sill, smiling and looking at my brothers in Christ, and He simply said "Well done, My good and faithful servants". This was an astonishing experience that has been etched deeply into my heart. I so clearly know how I need to serve and these two men provided great examples. They didn't feed five thousand people or provide a septic system for a county – they reached out to one person and that's all we need to do – share God's goodness and love.

It gets better. For some reason, I wanted to see Wayne M, our other deacon and good friend as he was someone that I knew could lift my spirits. Scott, Cindy, H.E. and Janis had been the arms and feet of Christ and were now gone. Mendi and I were in the room getting some rest and to my amazement, guess who comes prancing into the room – Wayne! How could that have happened? He was on my heart and as strange as this sounds, I wanted to hear from him and see him. God is good. I cried again as I was absolutely so overwhelmed that this divine appointment had just occurred. Wayne actually had just finished a twenty four hour shift at the fire house in Sugarland and drove all the way to Austin just to see me. That is insane. That is God's love. Later on Wayne became our lawn maintenance crew as he took over mowing our grass while we were gone. The poor fellow almost gave his life for us – he was stumbling around in our neighbor's shed for the mower thinking it was ours when the neighbor walked up on him – fortunately, no one was shot! We love Wayne and the whole family...Who was our welcoming home committee (the first time)? It was Wayne and his two boys who helped us un-pack and get settled in. Not only is Wayne doing God's work but his kids are seeing it first-hand.

For five days, they continued to siphon CSF using these two new drains which had been inserted into my back. Fortunately, my incisions were bone-dry by day five so they decided to remove the drains on the next morning and released me to go home.

4 GOING HOME, SORT OF...

As I recovered from this second surgery, we continued to deal with complications. I was regaining some coherence and even some appetite but the pain was still miserable. We at least saw some light at the end of the tunnel but it seemed that we kept bumping our heads along the way.

I wish I had a dollar for every I.V. stick I had. I believe at one point, they had tried nine different locations to start a new I.V. in my arms with no success. Even the floor expert was unsuccessful in getting a vein to stay open for the needle. Again I was crying but that was due to pain and dismay. I needed my I.V. for fluids and the pain medicine and we didn't know how to get out of this predicament. Fortunately, one of the nurses suggested to simply get a special order for a PIC line. Sure enough, around an hour later, this wonderful nurse came in, scrubbed up, created a sterile environment and placed an 18" catheter into a vein in my arm and ran it all the way over to the top of my heart. What a relief as I knew I no longer had to deal with any more sticks! Here's another lesson for me that was unraveling...Life is all about "Heart" – what's in our heart and then understanding the heart of God. For my ordeal with the I.V. sticks to be finally done with, we had to go straight to the heart...The heart of God is love. And His desire is for us to be in perfect communion with Him. For me to let go of the things that were so easily besetting me, I had to go straight to my own heart. The bible tells us that the heart is deceitfully wicked – that is until you've allowed Christ to enter in. The old has passed away and we are made new in Christ.

We were still dealing with the ups and downs of recovery and the cycle of not eating, no energy, getting sick, etc. But through all of this time, we each became prayer warriors relying on God to hold our hand through this. It clearly became a cleansing episode in my life as I continued to empty me of Dan and replace it with God's goodness and His Spirit. That is true healing, inside and out. Mendi continued to lift me up and encouraged me simply by reminding me to hold on to all of the hope that we have in a mighty and powerful God. She was an incredible witness to me as well as many others throughout this adventure. At one point though, Mendi had reached a low that was somewhat rare for her. She's a fighter and it's hard to get her down in the dumps. After a really tough episode of pain and incoherence, refusal to eat and vitals in terrible condition, Mendi shared with me that she had to the leave the room as she was overwhelmed. Watch out, another divine appointment is about to happen. Standing outside the door was one of our PA's, Charlie, the first person that I had met at the doctor's office who was assigned to also monitor my leak and recovery. Mendi simply fell into Charlie's arms and proceeded to break down sobbing. I thank God that He had Charlie standing there ready to take care of one of His children. By the way, Charlie is a she and wound up being a great support for Mendi during our stay in Austin. We actually had three primary PA's that were assigned to our case throughout our stay at the hospital and they each were wonderful. They were incredibly knowledgeable but more importantly, their bed-side manner was genuine and heart-felt.

I began searching for positives and good things to dwell on and of course many of my friends came to my mind and heart. Now, remember that I was still dealing with the impact of medicines and would occasionally visit "La-La land". One afternoon, I simply looked into Mendi's eyes and said "I miss Wu-Hao" with tears in my eyes. Three weeks later I learned from Mendi that she thought I was speaking gibberish. Interestingly enough, Wu-Hao is a very good friend at work. He is relatively new to our company but immediately I took a liking to him because of his calm and friendly nature and we've enjoyed many talks. I missed my friends.

I can remember the PA being so pleased with the current status as she had advised that if this hadn't worked, I would be facing surgery "# 3" and seven days flat on my back in ICU. Praise the Lord – I was finally getting out of Austin. Mendi transported me home in one piece on that Monday afternoon and even made a stop at Buc-ee's for a walk and a potty break. That evening, we enjoyed a home cooked meal provided by one of our church families. A few close friends came over that evening to welcome us home. There was still plenty of healing to occur, but the worst was over – or so we were thinking. On Tuesday afternoon, the day after being released, I went to lay down in bed for some rest and when I sat down, I realized that CSF was leaking out of my wound. I was devastated. I realized that the second patch had not worked and for the past week, the fluid had simply been pooling in my lower back area. What made matters worse was that I already knew what the next step had to be. I called Mendi and gave her the bad news and then called the doctor. They wanted us back up there immediately due to the complications related to losing this precious fluid. In my desperation to avoid the third surgery, we convinced them to allow us to wait until morning. Mendi and I prayed together that God would seal up the leak and that there would be no leak in the morning.

Our prayers were not answered (at least not in the way that we were hoping they would be at that moment in time) so we jumped back into the car and made a most miserable drive to Austin. At this point in the ordeal, I had realized that God was working on me and even Mendi and simply just wasn't done with the story that He was writing. I don't know why, but I did not shake my proverbial fist at God for another setback. Looking back at that episode now, I see that I was already going through changes that would allow me to be more Christ-like, as opposed to the controlling and domineering person I had been.

5 THIRD TIME'S THE CHARM

We arrived at the emergency room and I remember struggling to even get my legs out of the car. I was in immense pain, was sweating profusely and incredibly weak. With Mendi's help, I made it into the emergency room, then nearly passed out. One of the PA's that had been taking care of me met us there and had me re-admitted. We were in such distress, that neither of us packed clothes and I even had left my wallet at home. By this time, the staff knew who I was so no ID was required (I still had my first hospital ID bracelet on).

We both were whooped. No time to recover from being away from home for two weeks, barely able to walk, missing work, missing our family and we were staring at surgery # 3 and no less than 7 days flat on my back in ICU. We miraculously still were able to take this very disturbing predicament in stride and accepted it for what it was – another day in the valley of the shadow of death, but, no need to fear for the Lord was with us…we both were experiencing new levels of faith which actually in itself provided relief and comfort while facing this newest challenge.

Finally, that Wednesday, around 9:00pm, the neurosurgeon and patch specialist now has his turn at getting the leak to stop. Oddly enough, Mendi and Pops had the opportunity to visit with the doctor while he was catching a bite right before surgery. They also were surprised when the anesthesiologist walked in also wondering comically if I was in the surgery room all by myself. This surgeon specialized in the dura and the spinal canal and knew all of the tricks to get the patch to hold. We were told that when they had opened my incision (for the third time) that the CSF was leaking as if it were a geyser from one small area of the patch. They re-addressed the patch using a few tricks and then instead of using metal staples to close the incision, they used what they referred to as a "baseball" stitch to seal me up. The stitch work literally looked just like the seams on a baseball. This method was the best to use when dealing with fluid leaks. As far as I was concerned, they could have glued that incision if it would help to stop the leak.

They took me straight to ICU after a brief period in the surgical recovery room. I can recall that my very first ICU nurse simply had a very calming spirit and settled me in without much distress. That night, Austin was experiencing severe thunderstorms and we were having lightning and thunder that to me represented everything that I was going through. Incredibly, not five minutes after being rolled into ICU, the storm knocks out the hospital's power and I find myself desperately staring at a person who is a total stranger to me – what do we do now? No need to panic as all of my instrumentation was plugged into the red outlets which provided power from a battery back-up system. No need to fear.

Still being somewhat under the spell of the anesthetics, sleep came relatively easy. I woke up on Thursday with an incredible burden to bear as I realized this was day one of seven days flat on my back. This was really problematic for the "old Dan" – how can I be in control confined to a bed? How am I going to eat? I had question after question rolling through my somewhat fuzzy brain and they were all troublesome. Then something new and refreshing poured over my troubled spirit. With all of my heart and with total belief, I simply "advised" God that I was relinquishing the next seven days over to Him. I knew that I would not be able to handle this confinement as a man. In a sense, "advising" God actually makes no sense - we are in no way capable of advising God – he already knows everything. Furthermore, I was still figuring out that it wasn't the next seven days that he needed to handle for me…it was clearly the rest of my life. These revelations throughout the ordeal were so powerful that any pain that I was experiencing would become masked by the joy of knowing that God was on my side.

Time after time, I saw that I had to continuously step aside and make room for God to work. It is an emptying of one's self that allows the Holy Spirit to advise, instruct and to comfort. We can't do it on our own and we are ignorant of God's presence if we try to do anything with our own perceived strength. Three surgeries and I'm starting to see the proverbial trees through the forest. I'm really not a quick learner, but once I grasp onto a concept, I've got it – well, fortunately God was doing the grasping so these new concepts were certain to stick.

During the seven days on my back, I obviously had plenty of time to work through issues that I was dealing with and even unresolved issues from the past. With a new perspective related to the "appreciation of life", I was able to begin to process some difficult situations in much better light or should I say more clarity. I realized that my own faults sometimes mask the reality of situations and I needed to adjust and be more like Christ. In the middle of one particularly long night, I began to think about Jesus' disciple Peter and how he had actually denied knowing Christ three times, just as was predicted. Peter knew Christ and the others accusing Him also knew Peter well and knew that he was a follower of this Man that was now going to be sent to the cross. We see in the bible, and particularly in the Jewish culture that saying or doing something three times placed a higher degree of significance on the words or actions. The denial was clear the very first time and the corresponding message is also clear – we, the human race, are not capable of doing the right thing always. We will fail at some point. It is inevitable. Peter's three denials simply revealed the fallen nature of man with three exclamation points, not just one. We need a Savior. Here comes a great ending to this episode with Peter – Jesus very pointedly asks Peter "Do you love me" not just once but three times. This to me represents Jesus' forgiving nature and His desperation to restore a wandering sheep back into the fold. Jesus repeating His question three times also gave Peter the ability to re-affirm his love and commitment to Christ.

I began to change after the first surgery. I saw God moving and was realizing many flaws in my own character. I would have been content to get out of the hospital after the first one, but I believe that God had more to reveal to me and even to Mendi. For emphasis and for a dramatic flair, a third surgery would be necessary to complete this change that we were going through. It felt that with each surgery and with each level of desperation and despair, a better "Dan" was being cultivated – not a work done by me (or Mendi) but a work done by our Father God. Just like Peter, I believe that I needed three surgeries to yield the appropriate level of a wakeup call for my walk with Christ. Peter undoubtedly was agonizing in his own flesh and spirit as the words "no, I don't know Him" spewed out of his mouth. But, imagine the elation experienced when Jesus accepted three times a new and very meaningful "yes, I love You". I can honestly say that I am thankful for the experience that we had in September simply because I have been given the opportunity to grow in Christ and to tell Him three times that I love Him. I am no Peter and still need to grow more and more in my faith, but I see now that I am on the right path. Thank you Lord for the three surgeries.

I am thrilled to report that those seven days confined to the bed and on my back went by without a tremendous amount of difficulty. It was not fun, but it was manageable. God had provided Mendi, my precious and beautiful caretaker to be with me. He also filled those days with a very precious visit from my Mother from New Jersey, wonderful time spent with Pops and Karen (and great, healthy snacks from Karen!), a big surprise visit from my boss and visits from Marco, Gran and our church friends. One of the more memorable visits was little Macy from our church family who visited us with her Dad, Wayne M. Her precious presence in ICU visiting with us for forty five minutes provided such a lift for us. Finally, I also got to see Pastor Jack now that he had been cleared to travel to Austin (special permission granted by his daughter). I believe that everyone that came and carried us through this seven days were part of a divine plan that God had devised to take care of Mendi and me. It's not that Mendi and I were getting special treatment from our Creator. This love and care and grace and mercy is available to everyone and it's free. We just have to acknowledge it and allow Him to take control of our lives.

Finally day seven was here and it was time to remove the drains. We were confident that this third patch and the ensuing fluid pressure treatment "sealed the deal", literally and figuratively. So, our PA was there bright and early to remove the drains and to re-assign us to a regular hospital room. We stayed two more days in the hospital for observation and the leak had finally been conquered. Three surgeries, twenty four days in the hospital, a lot of tears and a lot of growing had all occurred. It was time to go home for good!

6 ANGELS, FAMILY AND FRIENDS

Remember to call on your Angels when you're in a jam – sounds too easy but you have to believe and real faith is believing without seeing (remember Thomas' doubt when Jesus had returned). There were a few times when I needed an angel, but I simply wasn't calling out for one. I believe that through Mendi's prayers and the prayers showered on both of us from family and friends, that angels showed up a few times without me asking them to and I thank God that they did.

Mendi is of course flesh and blood and is a member of the human race. But, in the month of September, it seemed to me that she was transformed into one of God's angels. We could fill up the Gulf of Mexico with all of the prayers that came from deep within her soul. Her faithfulness to not leave my side was un-wavering. The level of care that she provided for me could not have been bought with money. Her love which so wonderfully comes from the ultimate source of God's heart, strengthened me, enriched me and filled me.

There were so many facets of her love so similar to how a diamond shows off its beauty with every surface cut refracting and reflecting the beauty of light. She fed me. She prayed without ceasing. She lifted me up emotionally and encouraged me. If I ate a small morsel of food, she proudly proclaimed how excellent that was and then immediately had another bite ready for me. She held me so many times and this was extra special as I had gone several four or five day stretches without a bath. She coached me like a personal trainer teaming up with me to make the best of any accomplishment. She loved me despite my inabilities. I had created a situation where she was stuck in hospital rooms for three and a half weeks. She was terribly behind at work. She had lost all of the comforts of her home. She was in a place that she would have preferred to not have been in. But, without thought, she was automatically in the "being Christ with skin on" mode. What a beautiful and powerful display of unconditional love.

I will forever be indebted to her. Not surprisingly, she immediately pushes back any thanks as she indicates she was fulfilling her role as my wife and it was her privilege to take care of me. Wow!

There were two incidents that allow me to firmly believe that God will send His angels in time of need. Upon arriving back to the emergency room in a desperate condition and facing my third surgery, I really was at the lowest point of this entire episode. I was on the verge of passing out and was so distraught realizing that I would be in the hospital for another nine or ten days and seven of them flat on my back. I was ready to pass out and simply give up. I was barely able to sit in the waiting room and was on the verge of getting sick and blacking out. Then, to my astonishment, I perceived a nurse who may as well have had wings on, floating into my peripheral vision, then coming straight to me and asked "sir, would you like to lay down on that bed right there?" I was ready to throw in the towel. I was broken. I had no hope for that day or for the future. I was back in the Valley of the Shadow of Death. To this day, I believe that God sent that angel to me. She did not know why I was there. She did not know me. She did not know my condition. She came out of no-where. It was surreal. It was God.

That evening is when surgery # 3 took place and I spent my first night in ICU as they adjusted CSF (cerebral spinal fluid) pressure in my dura to aid in the sealing of the patch. You may recall that I literally had turned those next seven days over to God as I committed to him that I trusted him and would not rely on my own strength. That really was a smart move on my part – I need to consistently do this every day. Anyway, Thursday night right after shift changes for the nurses, I experienced another event and encounter that I can only attribute to the hand of God. A middle-aged African American nurse was assigned to my care for the next twelve hours. She was sharp as she jumped right in and made critical adjustments to the apparatus that was removing CSF from my spine at a rate of ten ccs per hour. She essentially took my vitals with her eyes closed yet, was delicate, caring and very interested in my well-being and comfort. She was different than the other nurses that had taken care of me for the past two weeks but I couldn't quite figure out why. I was in fairly decent spirits and was maintaining a positive outlook despite the entrapment of the ICU room and lying flat on my back. But, there remained a feeling of being challenged, not a challenge that I was having difficulty, but I knew that I was in a fight and that I needed every ounce of support, both heavenly and earthly, to finish strong.

With a steel determination, Sophia put up the blood pressure cuff, re-mounted the temperature monitor, turned to me and simply said, "Dan, would you mind if I asked you a personal question?" Immediately, I identified the difference – she was on a mission from God and she was to be my ICU angel. I told her yes, and in the kindest, non-invasive tone of voice, she simply asked me if I knew Jesus Christ as my personal Savior and Lord. I shared with her that not only did I know Jesus, but that I was relying on His strength and comfort to deal with the pain and recovery from three surgeries. She smiled from cheek to cheek and spoke a sweet "Praise the Lord". Just like Scott and H.E., here was another incident that God was smiling down and proclaiming "well done, My good and faithful servant".

I needed the reassurance that I was not alone and God used Sophia as an angel to drop in and say, "don't worry, the footprints in the sand are not yours, they're mine and I'm carrying you…" Sophia needed to go do a few other things and assured me that she would be back in to check on me. There's a feeling of warmth that I've come to know so much better now that fills me after recognizing God at work or God in our presence. I can remember growing up in my church back in NJ and old Neil getting up to the pulpit and simply exclaiming in his African American vernacular that "we all needs a li'l encouragement". Looking back, I realized that Neil was simply saying we need God to be our Motivator, Comforter, Caretaker and Friend.

Sophia revealed to me another facet of God's love. A few hours later, Sophia returned to my room for the last time during that shift and asked if she could pray for me and I without an ounce of hesitation said yes. It was an eerie setting as it was dark as it was in the middle of the night, but the typical monitor lights were flashing and here I was with this stranger grasping my hands so hard that they were numb. I had never been prayed for like this in my life. With every ounce of energy (or should I say simply in God's strength) she prayed for my continued healing, for comfort, for success of the third drain, for God to be with me and the prayer lasted perhaps for ten minutes. Why did she do this?

I really believe that she was an Angel. It gets better. Sophia finished praying for me and then looked me in the eyes again and asked me if I believed in being anointed with oil for God's healing to take place. I told her that I certainly believed in that but I was confused as to where she was going with this question. To my astonishment, she asked that if it were o.k. with me, she would anoint me with oil (sort of). Sophia held up a packet of Vaseline that the hospitals carry and explained to me that the Vaseline was petroleum or oil based and this is what she would use to anoint me for healing. I simply told her to please proceed. With the blessing of another prayer and with a complete humble and solemn heart, this precious lady anointed me with the Vaseline in the name of Christ and for God's healing power to come over me. This was perhaps the most moving and was certainly the most memorable moment of this entire episode. Sophia managed to convert the ICU bed into a precious altar where we were able to lay our burdens down and put on the yoke of Christ.

Over the next several days, Sophia would continue to pray for me and would become such an incredible blessing to me. She also would become a tool that showed me how I am to be for others. Paul tells us to be bold in our faith, in fact, be un-ashamed. She without an ounce of hesitation, and in a workplace, took somewhat of a risk to talk to me about Christ, to pray for me and to even anoint me with oil. That is bold and that again was Christ with skin on.

There were many others that weren't angels per se, but they acted as if they were angels. Cindy, our friend from church taxied Marco up to see us a couple of times and also brought up other friends and of course, Brother Jack and Ms. Ruth. Cindy's support, love and friendship that she offered to Mendi was invaluable. Janis, another faithful servant of God also was so instrumental in helping Mendi through her tough times. I have been blessed with great staff at work and their efforts during my absence were so much appreciated. They kept the ship afloat for sure. Pam's and Joann's faithfulness, prayers and support during the time away were so much appreciated. Kazzie and Vivianna would text me out of the clear blue sky to see how I was doing. All of my team at work did such a fantastic job that had provided such relief for me – everything was in good hands! Monta, Linda, Ms. Gail, Brother Barney and Ms. Joyce and the rest of the Adult Sunday School classes were prayer warriors lifting us up at every instance. Even folks that were relatively new to our community and church were praying and meeting our needs. Wayne S. reached out and cut the lawn right before a bridal shower scheduled months earlier that we had at our house on the first weekend after we were back home. He offered his help unconditionally.

The cards, letters, emails and texts from everyone at work, at church and from our families represented blankets of comfort that were undoubtedly necessary and clearly felt by both Mendi and me. The medical staff that we dealt with was awesome. The nurses genuinely provided care for me. Our PA's were precious, particularly as we struggled with the persistent leak. They were not just doing their job. They cared. My surgeons, all three of them were kind and competent and I am glad that I was referred to their office. Even our hospital doctor, Dr. B. was awesome – he was another Yankee like me, had a son in football and that provided many opportunities to share and to put pain on the shelf for a few minutes at a time – thanks Dr. B.

My Mom, Sarah Ann Martino, a proud resident of Westville, NJ for the last forty five years of her life was struggling as her "little Daniel" was not doing well. Mendi and the kids still tease me about the fact that my Mom still calls me Daniel and we all laugh about it. I'm glad that she calls me Daniel and glad that I have been blessed with a Mom that loves all of her children dearly. I believe that she would give her own life for one of us if it were ever necessary. My Dad died at age fifty three leaving my Mom and five of us kids behind. No insurance plan. No significant chunk of money anywhere. Just us. She made it work and I remain forever astonished by the actions that my Mom took simply to take care of us and to keep us together as a family. I learned an awful lot from her and the example she set during those trying times. Thanks Mom! On the third day of my ICU confinement, Mendi stepped away to get something from the hospital café in the middle of the afternoon. When she made it back to the room, she handed me a card that had my name (Daniel) written on the envelope. Instant tears again because not only did I know that the card was from my Mom, but I was prepared to bet my next paycheck that she was standing outside the door. And sure enough, she appeared with her bright smile and I was just overwhelmed. This surprise visit from my Mom was again instrumental in God's plan of seeing me through the seven days on my back. Thanks Mom for loving me, caring for me back home and then down here in Austin.

I can't forget to thank Marco, our fifteen year old, cuddly little son for how he took care of me and helped Mendi when we returned from the hospital (both times). It's a strange feeling to rely on your son to lift you out of a chair or to help you put on socks. It was humbling for me but at the same time, it was a wonderful opportunity for him to serve. Thanks Son, for your help and love that you showed to me and Mom during the past couple months. Kinsey was up at college so she wasn't present to help physically, but she provided support to both of us through her prayers, texts and phone calls...thank you Kinsey for who you are and for your love and support.

(I am certainly going to leave some people out accidentally as my brain was still in "reset" mode and I wish I could mention everyone that helped – I can just say thank you all and God bless you for reaching out to us!)

Later on the same day that my Mom surprised me, I was blessed with a complete surprise visit from my boss Joseph. I have been so fortunate with wonderful bosses throughout my career and Joseph is certainly no exception. He was kind enough to take time out of an incredibly busy schedule to come and visit me. His visit and kindness was extremely meaningful and went a long way in getting me through those long days lying on my back.

From day one on September 4th all the way through the last day, there were two people who became such integral parts of our lives that I could dedicate a complete chapter to them. Through every step of the journey, Mendi's Dad Eric and her step-mother, Karen were relentless in their support, affection, concern and love for the two of us. That might seem somewhat expected and not ridiculously out of the norm, but when you hear the "rest of the story", you'll see where I am coming from…

I met Mendi's Dad for the very first time only four years ago and since then, we've developed a really nice relationship. Prior to September, I had actually met Karen just two times – once for dinner with her, Pops and Mendi and once as they visited our home in Inez. That was it.

Sadly, Mendi and her Dad had some version of a disconnect that happened right before Mendi brought Kinsey into this world. Then for sixteen years, there was no contact between Mendi and Pops. There were perceptions of friction and misunderstandings that led to this separation. It always broke my heart as I had longed for a Dad but he had passed away. Mendi had her real Dad living only two and a half hours away, but there was zero relationship. Sad, confusing and unfortunate. I can remember driving through Austin many times with Mendi and her demeanor would always change as she continued to long for re-establishing a relationship with her Dad, as well as with Karen. Needless to say, Mendi would pray nearly on a daily basis that the reunion would take place and sure enough it did.

Around four years ago, I received a phone call from Mendi and all I could hear was sobbing. I did not know what was wrong with her. She had just received a letter from an Uncle (Pops' brother) that she hadn't talked to or seen in more than twenty years. He was writing to Mendi to advise her that her Dad wanted the opportunity to mend the past and to start over. Her prayers were working. I was thrilled that she was going to get her Dad back. Slowly but surely, they have nurtured their relationship back to a wonderful condition. The only difficult part over the past four years was that there was still un-certainty as to how Karen, Pop's wife was doing with this change in the relationship and both Mendi and I were feeling awkward as we wanted to get to know Karen better. It was just weird.

Here comes the crazy part of the story. Both Pops and Karen were at the hospital with us every single day. They cared for Mendi as if there had never been one single issue in the past. They cared for me as if I were their own son. Each day, the comfort became more special, more meaningful and incredibly valuable. Here was Mendi's step-mother not only providing motherly affectionate to Mendi, but also taking care of me as if we had known each other dearly for the past fifteen years. Like I said earlier, I had met Karen a grand total of two times prior to this event.

Pops and Karen provided relief for Mendi spending time with her at the hospital but also taking her out to eat just to catch a short break from taking care of me. The word "refreshing" comes to mind each time that I think of the love extended to Mendi and me from Pops and Karen. Where did the perceptions go? Where did blame go? Where did the past hurt and confusion go? To see the resiliency that Mendi, Pops and Karen displayed to strike out a chunk of the past and live in the present was another brilliant revelation to me that God was working in our midst. To see the healing of relationships occur right before your very eyes is precious. I am so glad to have an established relationship with Pops and Karen and they each hold a very special place in my heart. I could go on and on about the help that they provided us from medical advice (they are both doctors) to bringing me cinnamon espresso ice cream on particularly rough evenings. Since the event, our family actually went back to Austin and enjoyed precious time with Pops, Karen and Mendi's brother Christopher. I'm extremely fortunate to have two sets of in-laws. Thanks again Gran and Wayne for all you do for us. Thanks Pops and Karen for who you both have become in our lives! God is good, all the time and all the time, God is good.

7 A DESIRE TO SHARE AND TO CHANGE

So many people had been concerned about us that it was quite natural to share some aspects of "September" just to let everyone know that things were shaping up. Each time that we shared different parts of the story, it seemed that folks were moved, encouraged or intrigued. I started to think that perhaps I should capture some of the event on paper simply because it might provide some comfort or reassurance for others that are going through some tough times. I literally said "I need to write this story" three dozen times. One day I had the opportunity to share some of the events with a local pastor. While talking to him, tears rolled down his cheeks numerous times as he was moved by the fact that God is alive and well. I figured that if a pastor was being moved and perhaps even helped by this story, it would probably or possibly help others. Anyway, I committed to writing the story and "that's my story and I'm sticking to it".

Scott, our worship leader at church and also a good friend and one of our deacons had asked if I would be capable of sharing my story, more specifically, my testimony at church. I had only been home for a week but I was ready to proclaim God's goodness and to also begin the process of thanking so many friends and family members that had supported us. So, on the first Sunday in October, I had the opportunity to share our testimony with the church. There were many blessings for us as we were able to let everyone know that they had been so valuable to us and it turned out that the testimony wound up being a blessing to others.

A visitor that day had the opportunity to hear how God takes care of His sheep. This man had just learned that he had cancer and that the prognosis was not good. We continue to pray that he will call on God to be his Comforter, Caregiver and Healer. Here's the text that his sister-in-law sent us after we shared how God had been so present in our lives in September:

Hi. I wanted to tell you that your testimony yesterday was such a blessing. My brother in law is facing a huge surgery of removing a mass in his stomach. I believe God planned your testimony to be on the Sunday he came to church. I think seeing someone who was a Christian go through suffering, weakness and fear but cling to God to see victory was exactly what he needed more than a sermon. You had no idea he would be there but God did & you allowed God to use you as His vessel and you laid down your pride to share in your pain with everyone, through which we see God's mercy & grace & healing powers. My family prayed day & night for you, my heart was overwhelmed with a burden to lift you and Mendi up continually. I am so blessed and grateful for your healing and that you are using this to bring God glory. Thank you my brother, you were right, we are supposed to lift one another up & serve each other. We are blessed to have you & Mendi in our church family & as friends. Thank you so very much for your dedication to God and our church. My family is facing an unknown road but we serve a mighty God & healing belongs to Him. We love y'all.

Getting to see everyone again was almost like a reunion. The first person I saw was Na Naw, who nearly jumped for joy when Mendi and I walked in (She's an octogenarian but exudes the energy, excitement and joyous love of a teenager). She's our piano player at church, a matriarch, and one of the most loving people that we know. With her tears of joy, she welcomed us back. And then, one friend after another came up and hugged our necks and welcomed us back. It had been four weeks up in Austin but it felt like years. We were so thrilled to see ol' Brother Barney, Ms. Joyce, Ms. Gayle, Ms. Ruth, the Slatons, the Slatters, Bruce, Scott, Sherry, Tony, David, Tammy, Katy, Dan # 2 and on and on. We are so incredibly blessed. All of the Youth Group had sent us cards to lift us up. We had missed our Youth Group for four consecutive Wednesdays, so special thanks go out to the folks that stepped up and covered for us. We certainly need to thank everyone on Richter Road as we heard that all were praying for us. It's great to live in a community where folks are not ashamed to pray for one another. My brother and sisters are still up in NJ but kept up with our situation and supported us through the event. My youngest sister had gone through a similar back issue so she always had great advice for us and certainly understood our pain.

It is certainly necessary to know that each one of us is loved by God, but it's so beneficial to know that you are also loved by your family and friends. What's the point? Love someone today! We have all been given the innate ability to impact others positively. Can you imagine how much our world would change if we all took the opportunity to show love just like Na Naw showed to us? I remember that I'd always encourage Kinsey and Marco to "make someone smile today" each morning when we dropped them off at Aunt Susie's Schoolhouse. It really is that simple. Try it, you'll like it.

All of us have some testimony to share. Perhaps you lead a life that you weren't proud of but you finally turned over a new leaf. Maybe you've fought a battle, medical or otherwise, and you came through it. The old saying "been there, done that" has taken on a new meaning to me. My experience now offers me the inside look at a tough medical situation. I was put through the ringer, not just one time, but three times. I had lost decision making rights. I was on the edge of no return. I experienced a "hopeless feeling". But fortunately, I experienced God and He pointed me to my faith.

Recently, I was able to share some encouragement with a dear friend that is facing an incredibly tough battle with medical conditions. I was able to understand what she was going through and I was able to help her to deal with some of the issues. I would not have been able to do that so sincerely if I had not experienced the same conditions. A few days later, my phone rang at 11:30 at night and I remember thinking that something must be wrong for someone to be calling so late. Well it was my friend calling for comfort and prayer. I was so privileged to be in a position to help. Her pain was intense; she was having hallucinations and could not sleep. Because of my new and very personal experience in Austin,

I knew how to pray for her. I knew how to comfort her. God had granted me a bit more wisdom and insight as to how to help those in need.

Both Mendi and I were in need and so many reached out to us in love. It is now time to pay it forward. Thank God that I can help.

One of my brother-in-laws had gone through a four month battle quite similar to mine. As we received updates from my sister, I couldn't process what was happening. Her husband didn't want to eat or get up. He became lethargic and they too began to be concerned about losing him. Once I began to go through my issues, I began to more clearly understand what he was going through. I had reached out to my sister and him only occasionally and I now realized that I should have been much more diligent in my reaching out and with my prayers for them. My one-month ordeal was minor compared to his four-month ordeal. We've got to be prepared to reach out as often as possible and to share words of encouragement.

Christians are called to witness and to share the good news of Salvation and the Kingdom of God. Sophia reached out in an effort to share the "Good News" and the result was that she lifted me up when I desperately needed lifting up. She witnessed to me that God is alive and God is real and that God loves me. That singular event has inspired me to reach out more, to love more and to share my faith with as many people as possible.

I am not perfect (stating that just in case you thought I was). This entire event and all the words that I have written in this story do not make me perfect. What I am is forgiven. I have made tons of mistakes in the past and undoubtedly will make more mistakes in the future. This intense time that we had spent with God has reassured me that He is always there with arms wide open and that He will not forsake or leave us. We need to continue to strive to be holy but at the end of the day, the only way we can ever achieve that condition is through the blood of Jesus Christ. I've pledged to try my best to represent Christ in all that I do. That is also another way in which I am saying "thank you" to God for what he has done in my life and in Mendi's life.

Change is difficult. At work, the most rebelled against action is change. At church, we've sat in the same pew for years. We don't like change. But the concept of change was to be a major theme during my travails. I had become too reliant on my own strength. I was making "all of the calls" in so many aspects of my life. I was leaving God out of many decisions. I was not honoring God in my reactions to certain people or certain situations. I firmly believe that the three surgeries also were to show me that it was time for me to change. I needed a softer heart. I needed to cry more. I needed to rely on God more. I needed to be more forgiving (and forgetting).

I can only pray that the changes that have occurred in my heart already continue to develop and grow. I want to be humble. I want to help. I want to love. I now know that if God and His love are doing the leading, I will grow. I am not perfect and have dealt with my fair share of failures and sin in my life. I regret the sin but I have comfort knowing that I have been forgiven. I cannot erase the hurt that I caused in others, but I can pray for their forgiveness. I pray that moving forward, that I'll be much more successful in fighting temptation in this race here on Earth as I target the prize waiting for me when I get to my eternal home.

There were a few folks in my life that I simply chose to not fellowship with because of difficulties that I had experienced with them. I can remember lying on the hospital bed after the first surgery and these individuals were at the forefront of my mind. I actually became upset in my spirit as I went through a particularly difficult thought process – what if God chose to "not fellowship" with me because of my sin or stubbornness? I committed to God at that point that I would welcome those individuals back into my life and that I would strive to be as understanding as possible and to love like God as much as I could – unconditionally. The "**Judge not**, that **ye** be **not judged**" instruction from Jesus in the book of Matthew has taken on a whole new meaning…

Just a week or so after my release, I had to go back to the doctor's office to get my stitches pulled. These weren't ordinary stitches. They had put in a baseball stitch to seal up the six inch incision and to help fight back any CSF leaks. Anyway, one of the staff had informed us that she would be removing the stitches in my back. She also shared with Mendi and I that she really didn't like removing stitches nor did she like hurting patients and in fact, she had never removed this special "baseball" stitching. Of course, my eyebrows rose a bit and my level of anxiousness related to the pain jumped up a notch. I had already been through an incredible ordeal during the last four weeks – this certainly would be tolerable and a breeze.

Well, she started guessing her way through the pulling of the first couple stitches and with each subsequent pull, the pain worsened. Fortunately, the X-ray technician knocked on the door and advised us that she was ready to take X-rays of my back. Wow, saved by the bell (really by a knock). The office manager gave me the opportunity to finish up with stitch removal or to take a break. The old "Dan" would have said we're done and get someone else to finish the removal of my stitches. She was still in the first inch of six…The new "Dan" reacted to her question and humbly said, let's continue and get it done. Grin and bear it. Be humble. Don't be insulting in any way. It was the classic argument between the devil and the angel mounted on top of opposing shoulders. Fortunately, she suggested that we take a break and that I go get my X-rays. I breathed a deep sigh of relief. In just a few minutes I was back in the exam room on my belly waiting for her to return to finish the removal of the stitches. It did appear that she was learning as she went so I suppose that was a good thing. I heard the door open and much to my surprise it was my favorite PA and she was actually the one who put the stitches in. She grabbed the instruments and had all of my stitches removed in less than 30 seconds and pain free.

I sort of felt that I had accomplished a good thing that day. I did not hurt anyone's feelings. I did not become upset. I went with the flow. It all worked out in the long run. Another lesson – be patient and things will work out.

Changing is a personal challenge and for the most part, I am enjoying it. It feels good and right to let go of many things that controlled me or many things that I was supposedly controlling. This has been a refreshing period of my life and I plan to finish the race that I have begun looking toward that prize of hearing my God say "well done, My good and faithful servant". There will be times that I stumble and don't handle things in a proper way so I'll need much forgiveness and grace moving forward for sure.

8 WHAT'S NEXT FOR ALL OF US

I can only speak for myself. I want to be different. I have now developed this innate desire to reach out and help those in need. I believe that this is a simple response to all of the love that was directed toward Mendi and me. Making a difference or creating a smile actually requires minimal effort yet we too often neglect the opportunity. I was broken and severely humbled in many different ways during September. In this brokenness, I learned where I was failing and where I needed to change. This was in fact an incredible blessing.

In 2013 and into early 2014, we lost a good friend to Cancer. She and her family had fought a fight that lasted for more than one year. She did not make it. I fought my fight for 24 days. I made it. Every day that I was in the hospital, I reminded myself that I was still blessed. My problem was not a fatal one. I would survive. She fought every stage with incredible strength and faith. Her family was by her side each step of the way, adjusting their lives as necessary to support and love her through their battle with cancer. Looking back at what we observed, I now realize that they (Missy, her dedicated husband Allen and the two kids) actually taught Mendi and me how to fight and how to still be positive. Mendi and I would look at each other sometimes in our most desperate condition and we would share stories about our friend and how she fought. It was an instant reminder to us to keep fighting. She was a Champ in the truest meaning of the word and still inspires me to this day.

I remember one visit when Mendi and I ran up to Houston to visit her, I felt moved to encourage her to hold on to Christ. This turned out to be only a few days before she passed away. I had remembered the story about Laminin, an important protein in our body that helps to hold cells and tissues together. The shape of this protein is what makes this story very interesting. The protein is many times found in the shape of a cross. The story has been around for a while, but it is incredibly appropriate that this protein that holds much of our body parts together is shaped like a cross. Without Christ on the cross, we not only fall apart here on Earth, but are doomed to a dark and painful eternity. My last words to her were to cling to the cross and all that it stands for. Jesus died on that cross for you and me, but rose triumphantly now standing in the gap for us. I will be forever grateful to this family for showing me how to fight valiantly, despite the challenges.

For Mendi and me, September's journey basically had the same impact that a Vow Renewal ceremony might have. In that one month, we grew closer than we have ever been. She taught me with her word, actions and tears what real unconditional love of a spouse is. God and our faith was planted right back in the very center of our relationship. We both fundamentally believe that we need to place God first before each other and that has provided many blessings for us.

I would ask everyone that has taken the time to read this story to reach out in love at every opportunity that presents itself. Sometimes it's just a phone call. Other times, you might be significantly inconvenienced. It's ok. Remember the inconvenience that Jesus went through on the cross for us was incredibly significant. Effective and meaningful giving truly requires some sacrifice on the giver's part. Go out of your way to make a difference in someone's life.

I'm glad to have written this story – I'll need to read it every once in a while to keep me centered on who I want to be in Christ. There are many things that occurred in the hospital that Mendi tells me about of which I have absolutely no recollection. Yes, things were that bad. I am certain that I've forgotten to thank someone special so I need to just put out another special blanketed Thank You to each and every person that prayed, called, texted, hugged, mowed grass, cooked great meals and simply blessed us with their kindness during our tough times. You made a significant difference in our lives and we are deeply grateful for that.

God, thank You for the chastening and the love that you shared with me in September. Thank You for sending Your Son and for sending the Comforter.
Mendi, thanks for being my wife and for genuinely showing your unconditional love for me.
Gran and Grand Dad, thanks for being there for us always and of course for taking care of Marco.
Mom, thanks for being my Mother. I would want it no other way. And thanks for your visit.
Pops and Karen, thanks for each and every minute that you shared with us in September and thanks for being in our lives.
Kinsey and Marco, thanks for the love that you showed me and Mom during this tough time.
Brother Jack, thanks for the phone call as it will never be forgotten.
Pam, Joann and the rest of my staff, thanks for holding the fort down, as simple as that!
To my sisters and brother back in NJ and my sisters and brothers in Christ – without you all, it would have been so much tougher. Thanks for being who you are.
Missy, Allen, Hannah and Logan - thanks for teaching us how to fight.
 To everyone else, thanks for allowing Mendi, Kinsey, Marco and me in your lives.

<u>Here's the most important message that I can leave with you:</u>

John 3:16King James Version (KJV)

[16] For God so loved the world, that he gave his only begotten Son, that whosoever believeth in him should not perish, but have everlasting life.

ABOUT THE AUTHOR

Dan was born on March 19th, 1962 to Ernest Louis and Sarah Anne Martino in Philadelphia, Pennsylvania (christened as Daniel Martino having the full name of Daniel as in "the Lion's Den" Daniel and with no given middle name). Later on in life, he was given an unofficial nickname of Marco, as in Marco Polo, the Italian world traveler and explorer. He was born into the "Church of Our Lord and Savior Jesus Christ", a non-denominational, Bible-preaching church. He was the third child of five children including one older brother, Ernest, one older sister, Theresa and two younger sisters, Rachael and Kathleen. Dan also has a half-sister Marcella from his Father's first marriage. The family lived in an old Italian neighborhood in South Philadelphia until 1968 and then moved to Westville, NJ, a small town right by the Delaware River and only fifteen minutes from Philadelphia. Dan lost his Father at age 13 to Hodgkin's disease. Everyone in Dan's immediate family still resides in South Jersey.

Dan attended elementary school in Westville, NJ and attended Gateway Regional High School in Woodbury Heights, NJ and graduated in 1980. He attended Rutgers University for three and a half years but never obtained a degree. After leaving college, he was working for a custom in-ground pool company and also enjoying the opportunity to coach youth football. Eventually, a significant employment opportunity came along with a company called Nan Ya Plastics, a Taiwanese plastics company which had several various operations here in the United States. This new position led to an opportunity in 1989 to take a job transfer and move to Texas and work for Formosa Plastics USA, a sister company. In 1992, he transferred seven miles north to Inteplast Group, a new downstream plastics manufacturing company where he still is employed.

Dan is married to Melinda (Mendi) Kaye Martino, originally of Edna, Texas. He has one step-daughter, Kinsey Deanne, currently studying at Sam Houston State University in Huntsville, TX and a son, Marco Daniel, a freshman at Industrial High School in Vanderbilt, TX.

His willingness to serve is evident as he has spent numerous years in many different organizations. Dan has served as a director, and in most instances, an officer for the Jackson County Chamber of Commerce, Emergency Food and Shelter Program, Industrial Education Foundation, United Way of Jackson County and several others. He also has been very involved with church related activities and is currently a Deacon, Treasurer and Music Minister at First Baptist Church Inez. He continues to enjoy his trumpet as he has been playing for more than thirty five years. Music is his favorite hobby and he enjoys singing, playing the guitar and playing the piano.

Dan and his family reside in Inez, Texas appreciating life in a community where God is still present.

37683360R00031

Made in the USA
Charleston, SC
17 January 2015